About the Author

Born in 1942, married to Denise for fifty-four years, two sons, Jason and Craig, internet provider, office fit out contractor. Currently semi-retired, not by choice, after COVID-19!

Enjoys motor cruiser weekends March to November. Swims five-hundred metres on weekdays, shoots clay pigeons and occasional game, enjoys eating out and owns an apartment in Northern Cyprus. Freeman of the City of London.

One Thing Leads to Another

Brian S Lamden

One Thing Leads to Another

Olympia Publishers
London

www.olympiapublishers.com
OLYMPIA PAPERBACK EDITION

Copyright © Brian S Lamden 2022

The right of Brian S Lamden to be identified as author of this work has been asserted in accordance with sections 77 and 78 of the Copyright, Designs and Patents Act 1988.

All Rights Reserved

No reproduction, copy or transmission of this publication may be made without written permission.
No paragraph of this publication may be reproduced, copied or transmitted save with the written permission of the publisher, or in accordance with the provisions of the Copyright Act 1956 (as amended).

Any person who commits any unauthorised act in relation to this publication may be liable to criminal prosecution and civil claims for damage.

A CIP catalogue record for this title is available from the British Library.

ISBN: 978-1-80074-152-2

First Published in 2022

Olympia Publishers
Tallis House
2 Tallis Street
London
EC4Y 0AB

Printed in Great Britain

Foreword

Towards the end of boring Coronavirus lockdown, but having thought about it for a long time, I decided to write the story of my life. As I say, I'd been thinking about it for a long time but didn't think it would be of interest. As I went through writing notes, I was surprised what I had achieved and maybe others might also be interested. I only thought about this title as I was going through the writing of notes and did realise how things had run on from one to another, largely by accident. I would like to thank many, in some ways, and dedicate this to a number of people. Firstly, my wife Dee who has put up with me for fifty-four years, bought up two boys but largely on her own, as I was always working, leaving early and arriving home late; almost always just to go to bed. Also, she was a tremendous help and support when I was President of the Building Surveying Division of the RICS and also as Master of the Worshipful Company of Chartered Surveyors. I would also like to thank all of those that I have worked with, partners, friends, employees and especially the team at Hillier Parker. They were a great team and I still see some of them for a beer from time to time. Also over the decades, various typists, secretaries, personal assistants and so on, all very long suffering and in particular Susie Bevan who still does some work for me and in fact is typing this draft. She has worked with me at Hillier Parker and onwards through Brian Lamden Associates for in excess of twenty-five years. All long suffering. Thanks.

I have often said I was born to be a Building Surveyor and certainly look after clients but in fact, it was a while and indeed a few other ideas before I actually embarked upon the building surveying professional route. I was born in 1942, therefore being a war baby, and I am still sort of kicking and working, when I get the chance, and indeed as I started to dictate this, I've just received an enquiry to quote for a survey of a farmhouse in Cookham. The first quote since the virus started and indeed the first quote for some time, so who knows. Being born during the war years, and living with my parents and grandparents near Windsor, I do have some wartime memories. I can recall being taken out on to the balcony of the flat where we lived and seeing a thousand bomber raid going overheard on its way to Germany and also from the same vantage point, seeing in the distance the glow of London burning during the blitz.

At some time, I know not when or why, mother and I were evacuated to Bexley Heath. Parents had some friends there, the connection of which escapes me and for some reason it was felt safer there, rather than between Windsor and Ascot, although I can't see why it would be safer to be in Greater London, especially as the house we stayed in, in Bexley Heath, had a large electricity pylon in the garden. I guess then the supposed radiation from high level electricity transmission lines was not considered seriously and I'm not aware of any after effects.

We did, however, suffer a close shave with a bomb. I was in a pram in the garden, and have been told I was showered with brick bats. Not the first of many incidents of that during my career. We did have a makeshift air raid shelter which I recall was some form of table in the kitchen into which I was bundled when the sirens went off.

Being a Building Surveyor, I was often referred to by less educated and qualified General Practice Surveyors and viewed as a 'brickie'. Most of those former colleagues still don't understand what a Building Surveyor is or does. I can in fact, recall a partners meeting at Hillier Parker when there was reference made to producing drawings that one eminent partner and great friend of mine stated 'we don't do those do we, I thought we left those to architects'. I always had to fight hard for recognition, status, referrals and proper fees. It was a fight but I was generally lucky with discussions with partners and colleagues. As Chartered Building Surveyors, however, we are still having the same debates with the RICS, having gained the status of a Division and been very successful (perhaps that's the problem, too successful). Whilst the title of Chartered Building Surveyor still exists, its status in the RICS hierarchy has been totally dissipated and indeed at the present time, virus excepting, there is a bit of a resurrection of a revolution to create a separate building surveying organisation. The thread of building surveying and its relationship with others will pop up from time to time in this story. By the way, I have never been a diary writer so recollections, names and some dates are all from memory and therefore apologise for any minor inaccuracies.

So how did I start? Although not obvious in my early

years, I have always said I was born to be a Building Surveyor and to serve clients and as it turns out, whilst I never made a fortune, I did reasonably well with few hiccups and happy to be called a brickie, albeit the chartered brickie.

Pre-school and at junior school, we lived in a flat with my grandparents on a large estate. My grandfather was sort of an odd job man come dogs body, come chauffeur to Lord and Lady Austin on their estate at Fernhill Park, Ascot. This is now owned by an Arab and it is a stud farm. The flat was in the courtyard of the garage and general stables area to the mansion.

Fernhill Park is a Grade 11 listed Mansion set in 200 acres of parkland with adjoining farmland and a farm complex on the edge of Windsor Great Park .The original house was built before 1700 but modelled in the early 17th Century by the Architect John Thorpe It was the last Berkshire home of the Knolly's family descendents of Sir Francis Knolly, Treasurer to Queen Elizabeth1's Royal Household.

Is it too much of a coincidence that the Company, of Watermen and Lightermen of the River Thames (see later) have resurrected a ceremony, Knolly's Rose which is the payment of a "quit rent" dating back to1383 and is the payment of a red rose to the Lord Mayor of London which is a fine for the wife of Sir Robert Knolly building a foot bridge from their house in Seething Lane to their garden opposite.

Later owners of Fernhill Park included Charles Theophilus Metcalf, later Lord Metcalf, former Governor- General of India, Jamaica and Canada. Not all at the same time.

Colonel Waite was an Australian racing driver. He served in Gallipoli, where he met his wife Irene, the daughter of Baron Austin the founder of the Austin Motor Company. Needless to say whilst Baron Austin made the cars, Colonel Waite made them famous. He raced an Austin 7 at Brooklands and won the 100 mile road race at Phillip, Island in Victoria State which was officially recognized as the first Australia Grand Prix. For a while he ran Austin Australia, was also awarded The Military Cross and became a member of the Order of St Johns. There is an interview of him on u tube.

The only real memories of Fernhill Park was at the bottom of the Lawn was a wood with a nearby lake and swimming pool We used to walk in the woods .I don't know how it happened, whether fishing or what but Dad lost his wedding ring in the lake. The lake wasn't small but they drained it and after a lot of searching the mud Dad found his ring. The other memory was the swimming pool. Quite large, probably 20 yards long. It was only used by guests during Ascot week which is just up the road. Grandfather spent most of the year cleaning it by hand, using razor blades Not sure it was used. We were not allowed to use it even when the Waites were away. From Fernhill Park I attended the local Primary school, Cranbourne County Primary School. I don't think I was too keen to go in the beginning as I can remember my mother telling me that I just held on to the railings screaming my head off .I think Dad left me and they persuaded me to go in.

Don't have too many vivid memories but can

remember the buildings with a sports field behind .From what I saw as I drove past a few years ago it seems very much as it was. Can recall athletics and playing football. I think to begin with I was dropped off by Dad and collected by Mum. I also remember later cycling and back home probably via the woods or the farm. I guess we were a couple of miles from home.

Looking through my school reports I seem to have started at 5 years old. I can remember the Headmaster Mr. Andrews, good and fair Also the Assistant Head Mrs Rendell who, probably unfairly because of her age was referred to as "granny", all grown-ups were old, to us kids.

Mrs. Rendell seems to have been our form teacher for a while until my last year when Mr. Calderbank took over. By coincidence Mr.Calderbank had a brother scientist who also worked at Jealott's Hill. Academically I didn't do too badly, generally in the top quarter of the class of around 40, got promoted to the "A" stream. Reports generally stated I was intelligent but untidy and impatient and often reported" could do better and sometimes has a don't care attitude.

In 1954 I passed the 11 plus and gained a place at Windsor County Boys School. The Grammar School.

Dad worked at the ICI Research Station at Jealott's Hill near Bracknell. He started from school when the station consisted of two sheds and his job was office boy, cleaning out inkwells and he went right on until retirement to become Company Secretary and Administrator to what had then become a large research station with hundreds of employees. Currently there is a planning application and appeal to develop 200 acres for 2000 houses. I guess early on in life and certainly when I went to Windsor Grammar School, we had moved to an ICI flat in a converted, large building at Binfield and then to our own house in Wokingham. In my early, young days, whilst living at Fernhill Park, the courtyard was the centre of deliveries, builders mess rooms, my grandfather's workshop and so on and with builders coming and going, I got to know them, used to join them for breakfast and coffee and got to know their ways and their language! I even helped out with my own wheelbarrow, undoubtedly, being more of a nuisance than assistance but I was certainly part of the gang.

By the time we moved to Binfield and on to Wokingham, Dad was moving up the Jealott's Hill ladder, becoming Assistant Secretary as the research station grew and grew. There was an experimental farm with a dairy herd and also for the 'Plant Protection' side of ICI (subsequently to become Astra Zeneca) arable plots for research into fertilizers, weed killers and so on. In an old mansion on part of the site, known as Hawthorne Dale, there were offices and laboratories. I can vividly recall rooms with cages where they bred locusts and other insects for experiments. They also grew various plants for experiments in greenhouses adjacent and used, what we would probably now call grow lights which were on 24 hours and enabled the station to be visible for miles around.

In 1993 ICI demerged leaving Zeneca Agro Chemicals and Novartis Agro which became Syngenta as it is now.

In his role as assistant secretary, Father was regularly involved in the maintenance of the buildings together with alterations, repairs and new construction which, over the years, were considerable, including new chemical laboratories and so on and as the station grew a new canteen block. I took an interest in all of his work and often visited the station with him.

I can recall, at an early age, probably around when I started at Windsor Grammar School, joining the annual harvest of the experimental plots.

The experiments were set out in plots which were probably 10 yards square or so. They were planted with grasses and corn and wheat and each plot was treated differently with different fertilizers or chemicals and differing amounts, which were all monitored. Come harvest time, an old fashioned reaper and binder, tractor drawn, was used. The crop from each square plot was separately harvested and bound into sheaves of corn and the product from each plot, once stooked and dried and wrapped in a large hessian sheet, with one sheet per plot were then collected by tractor and trailer and stored in a barn until it was time to dry the grain and then the grain, straw were then all measured for experimental purposes, the amount of yield and so on.

At an age when I was certainly not licensed to drive and there were public roads that ran through the station, I found myself driving a Ferguson tractor with a trailer, collecting these bundles from the fields to the barn. On one occasion, I actually ran myself over with a tractor when a colleague coming the other way, threw a bag of sweets which landed short in front of the tractor. When I got off the tractor to collect them, I forgot to knock it out of gear and found the front wheels running over my leg. I was obviously young and supple, let alone somewhat surprised and suffered no injury.

There was a local contractor firm in Bracknell, who were employed as contractors on the site, both employed as regular maintenance contractors, dealing with repairs and decorations etc. as well as alterations, refurbishments and so on and some larger scale work. Father introduced me to this firm, John C Sargent Limited and certainly in the early years at Grammar School to earn pocket money, I used to work for them, initially on Saturday mornings only but then school holidays and so on. John C Sargent was a family business, owned and run by two brothers, one of whom had two sons, Peter and Michael who, with a couple of other directors, basically ran the business.

As was the case in those days, it was traditional for contractors to also be Funeral Directors and Ted Sargent, one of the older owners basically concentrated on this side of the business. There was a consecrated Chapel in the builders' yard, next to the cement shed, although for clients as Ted lived on the main road adjacent, there was a client entrance to the Chapel via his house and garden. From time to time, as I grew a little older, I occasionally ended up assisting deliveries to the Chapel from the Dormobil which collected deceased clients, day and night and embalmed them in the Chapel.

As I grew up, I continued working every hour available at weekends, holidays etc. for pocket money.

I started in the carpenters' workshop, tidying up, sweeping up shavings etc. and graduated to making coffins. This is actually quite easy with pre-cut boards with partial depth cuts in the inside of the boards at 'shoulder height'. This allowed them to bend around the shoulder area. Much easier for cremation coffins as they are covered in purple felt with wooden handles etc. and no varnish. On one occasion, after having my sandwich lunch in the coffin shop which was a mezzanine to the carpenters shop, I decided to have a kip in one of the boxes we had made that morning, only to find that my colleagues decided to put the lid on. They were quite comfortable actually with a calico lining and a sawdust base, not just to make it comfortable but also to soak up bodily fluids!

As I gained a few years and became more and more involved in the business at weekends and holidays, firstly I think I became a plumbers mate. On one occasion at East Hampstead College, there is a large old house converted to a Ladies College, I spent most of the day at the top of a 100-foot single pole ladder (a hayrick type of ladder) holding up (held by rope as well) a very large ornamental lead rainwater hopper head to allow clearance of the blocked rainwater pipe. Over one Christmas period with a very heavy frost, I spent lots of overtime working, assisting a plumber, defrosting homes. Incoming cold water mains were quite shallow in those days, generally of lead or galvanised iron piping and froze easily so we had to dig up gardens and thaw them out. Sometimes, the frozen pipes were internal and less efficient than current central heating, certainly less insulation. I recall one particular large house just on the outskirts of Ascot which was frozen up solid and we worked internally in the roof space and elsewhere trying to thaw it out. We had a gismo which was, I guess, basically some form of transformer which was quite heavy with the mains connection and two leads with forked prongs on the end of each and we used to put these on the pipes and obviously pass electrical current between the two ends. This would thaw the ice in the pipes. This particular property was seriously frozen up and by midnight Jack, the plumber I was working with, and I had enough, having been up at about 6.00am and decided to go home and return the next morning. We therefore left the family with only partially thawed pipes. We arrived next morning, bright and early, to find water cascading down the stair carpet. We had obviously done sufficiently to partially thaw the pipes and for them to start running during the night. Obviously, we had left the taps open to see when they thawed and of course they flowed but the waste pipes were still frozen, so there was nowhere for the water to go other than down the stairs. I recall the lady of the house was remarkably calm when we arrived.

Earned a lot of pocket money that Christmas.

Then I think I was promoted to the stores and became the store keepers' mate. The stores kept quite a collection of building materials, screws, nails etc. as well as plumbing materials and so on. We had accounts with local builders merchants and in those days of course, before computers and computer stock control, you could generally find something in the builders merchants yard. In those days lots of drainage was cast iron 'LCC' drain ware and for sure somewhere in the long grass, if you needed one, you could probably find a 97 ½ degree cast iron bend! As a storekeepers mate, I was a jack of all trades, often assisting loading of lorries. We kept stocks of sand and ballast in the yard and had a loading tractor which was simply a Fordson tractor with a high lift front bucket and we'd use that to load lorries. On one occasion as we had a site of old people homes being built, half a mile away from the yard (it's still there), they needed a cubic yard of ballast and the simple answer was to dig the shovel into the heap in the yard and drive it up the road. Being a very inexperienced driver but always on full throttle, it didn't' cross my mind that the ton of ballast up in the air slightly relocated the centre of gravity of the tractor and it was with some surprise as I roared round the Downshire Way roundabout that I found one of the rear wheels off the ground ,but it went back again!

Being in the yard was also a question of unloading deliveries. On one occasion at lunch time, we had a cement delivery and being a fit, athletic sort of guy, on a hot summer day, I single handedly unloaded 20 tons of CWT bags of cement. Because it was hot, I didn't have a shirt on and regretted that after I had finished because the strong cement paper bags didn't agree with my bare shoulder.

From the base of the stores and obviously by then being 18 and a qualified driver, I became a part time lorry driver. Indeed I had my own lorry which was only used by me when I was working. This was a very old-fashioned petrol Ford, probably thirty hundred weight tipper lorry which had come with Sargent's purchase of another small contractor, I think Ernest Brown in Bracknell. It was a rattily old vehicle but used to go a bit and seemed to be quite busy when I was available. Needless to say, my erratic driving gave rise to a few amusing incidents. On one occasion, I was delivering bags of cement to the Road Research Laboratory in Crowthorne (where I saw Sterling Moss testing a Ferguson four-wheel racing car on the skid pan). I also took a Dormabile around the banking on the test circuit and had a struggle keeping it down the banking at full throttle. Anyway, following the delivery of cement, I was back in the yard when one of the other drivers asked if I'd been to the Road Research Laboratory in the afternoon. I said yes, why. He said did you lose a bag of cement (I was driving the lorry without the tailboard up). I said I didn't realise that and he said, well you did because when I went round there was somebody with a bucket and spade clearing up the cement from the road. In the same lorry and we were building the National Employers Mutual office, I think, in Ascot, we were using bricks from the now defunct and disappeared Bracknell brick and tile works, I spent a number of days and probably moved five-thousand bricks a day from inside the kiln (very hot and dusty) on crowding barrows which are very unstable barrows used to carry the clay from the clay pit to the kiln and which fell over if you didn't load the bricks evenly, onto the lorry which took a thousand at a time. At the same time, I collected a large piece of skirting board from that site to go back to the yard for moulding in the carpenters shop but it never reached the yard. I just poked the bottom end of the fairly flexible long piece of timber under the tail board and rested it over the bolster, which is the frame over the cab where you used to put ladders I didn't bother to tie it on and driving with my usual gusto, it was quite springy and it just whipped off the back. By the time I'd realised that it had gone, stopped the lorry and gone back, somebody had appropriated it and taken into their back garden!

Having the lorry was often quite hard work and in clearing sites, I'd often end up loading by hand a ton of brick rubble and so on into the lorry for tipping into a landfill. One of our runabouts, which took men to sites, was an old Dormabil van and we used that for delivering materials to sites as well. On one occasion, I went to the builders merchants to collect a gallon of light blue paint. Again in the summer with the sliding doors wide open, I swung around a roundabout in Bracknell where the gallon of paint decided to go its own route, through the sliding door. For quite a long time, there was a trail of blue tyre marks up Bracknell high street. More than once I borrowed the Dormabil for my own personal use, driving a young lady up to the cinema and dinner in Soho and parking the Dormabil on a meter and on one occasion with my school cadet hat on, a number of us borrowed it for a night exercise on the Berkshire Downs and I can recall chasing rabbits in the headlights but we didn't have any ammunition for the Lee Enfields we carried with us. The most exciting escapade was driving another of our vehicles, a thirty hundred weight van and towing a large

Muirhill rear wheel steering dumper. Again I think to the Road Research Laboratory. I was towing with only a chain around the side roads between Bracknell and Crowthorne and it has to be said probably not driving that slowly. The guy driving the dumper, it turned out, wasn't used to rear wheel steering (which means you turn the opposite way to the way you want to go) and was weaving all over the road behind me. At one particular point, we met a large lorry coming in the opposite direction. This lorry was loaded with sacks of potatoes which, if you'd seen these lorries, you will realise that the sacks often protruded beyond the side of the open sided lorry. Of course just as we came alongside each other, the dumper decided to swing out past the van. The dumper skip caught the nearest row of potato sacks neatly, ripping them open and at the same time tipping the skip up, depositing the contents of a forty-gallon drum of diesel on the road to mix with the potatoes. Not much we could do apart from pick up the empty diesel drum and leave somebody else to sort out the potato mix!

As a sort of spare man in the stores and with a driving licence, I often drove a variety of vehicles including the fore runner of a JCB, road rollers etc. and I remember on one occasion on a site in Wokingham where we were building a new car park, a lorry got bogged down, the digger sent to pull it out got bogged down, the road roller sent also got bogged down and they all stayed together for more than a few days until the weather dried out and they could be pulled out sensibly. Needless to say, I think I was the driver of the lorry that first got stuck.

Another amusing incident was not related to driving.

As I've mentioned, the firm were also funeral directors and that included digging the graves. This job was usually done by a labourer who was well versed in digging six foot long holes and did it by hand on his own on most occasions. In one particular situation, however, he cried for help. He was digging a grave at a parish church in Binfield in very foul weather. He had a petrol driven pump and that was just about coping but getting near to the funeral hour, he was really struggling and I was volunteered to give him a hand. I duly got on my pushbike and joined him with another spade and with difficulty and the pump at full blast, we finished the grave. It was, however, filling with water rapidly so we kept the pump running until the funeral cortège arrived in the distance and pulled it out and then hid behind some gravestones until they went into the church. By arrangement with the Verger, who was going to signal when the funeral was over so we put the pump back in until they started to leave the church, pulled it out and hid again. As soon as the burial was over and the mourners turned their backs on us, we promptly shoveled clay, madly, onto the coffin, stood on it to stop it floating out and eventually truly buried it. So apart from being a pall bearer, I know a bit about funerals. We had our own limousines and hearses, again in the yard and usually parked in the cement shed when not being used and pall bearers were a mixture of lorry drivers, plumbers, brick layers and so on, seconded for the occasion, all generally wearing their pin stripe trousers and waistcoats etc. on the site until they had to put their black jackets on.

Whilst I was filling my leisure time with these

activities, I was full time at Windsor Grammar School. I was a keen athlete, indeed County Quarter Mile Champion at one stage. During the summer season, I would spend five or six days, including Sundays, training in the evenings at the Bracknell athletics track and competing on a Wednesday afternoon and/or Saturday. I was an all-round athlete (believe it or not) and on a Saturday would often compete in six different events from high jump, quarter mile, hundred yards, the mile and wherever we were short of athletes. The Bracknell Stadium was built by Sargents and in those days, consisted of a running track, field events areas and jump pits and a small grandstand with changing rooms under. As Sargents had been involved in it when it was officially opened, there was an opening athletics event, in which I competed with minor internationals shall we say. I was amused, having spent most of the previous days with a paint brush in my hand and finishing off the grandstand to hear one American athlete say 'gees, this is a fantastic place they even flush the johns with hot water!. What nobody realized was that was not design but there had been a bit of a misconnection of plumbing or, as I now suspect, an overflow of expanding hot water from cylinders to the cold-water storage.

As I say, I spent a lot of time at the track in the summer, not only training but there were a number of female athletes to talk to!

In my time, our coach and chairman attracted one or two notable athletes and I trained with Mary Bignell (later Mary Rand) an English team athlete, Stan Eldon who was a distance runner for England, with whom I used to run road running and cross country in the winter, who coincidentally ran a sports shop in Reading subsequently and came across one or two other GB athletes such as Gordon Pirie and so on.

Of course, I carried out all of these athletic pursuits at school and also played at school for the first rugby team. Not content with that, I joined Bracknell Rugby Club. This was the local rugby club, possibly but I don't recall, in a local league but at the age of 14, I recall when I first joined, I was a bit of a lightweight in a grown men's team, hence I cracked my ankle, playing for them when a rather large fullback tried to stop me (and succeeded) in scoring a try and sat on my ankle with a loud crack. Still I recall with physio, going on a school skiing trip about six weeks later so it wasn't too serious.

Subsequently, after I left school and obtained my first car (a Fiat 600) I continued to hone my driving skills from dumpers and JCBS, joined, and became a member of the Bracknell Motor Club, eventually Chairman.

This was in the good old days and we used to rally on public roads, including all night rallies, roaring around the local countryside, keeping the residents awake and so on but that eventually was stopped, although I did hold a restricted RAC driving licence for a while and navigated and drove, both on restricted rallies and a few little sprints in a friend's TR4 at Silverstone and Brands Hatch.

That was a bit later in life when Dee and I were engaged. I competed at Silverstone in the TR4. The competition included now classic cars, a Daimler Dart ,2 Aston Martin Zagattos and an ex Le Mans Ferrari 250

GTO. A little outclassed on the first lap, I spun at Woodcote(the old course) and it wasn't until after, talking to Dee after I had finished I discovered that not only did I spin but she told me that I had spun as the Ferrari was overtaking.

Back to Bracknell Motor Club, four of us went to Le Mans in the days of the Ford GT40's domination We went in a Morris 1100 (sort of a large mini). Left Bracknell early on Friday evening returning back early on Monday in time for work. Cooked breakfast on the side of the Autoroute. On Saturday slept on the grass in the car park. Oh to be young again. We have been back once more but slept in hotels, generally too noisy for Dee.

At Windsor school, academically, I was fairly diligent, but only fairly. Beyond school work I was always enthusiastic about becoming outside of the classroom. I was in the "A"stream but not the best there. It was suggested that I gave up Latin after a first year score of 16%. French followed not too long after .At some stage however I was 5th in class. I seemed to remain 5th in class although reading my reports sometimes it is difficult to believe.

Generally "satisfactory" to the odd "excellent" conscientious and deserves success. Best subjects History, Geography and for some strange reason Religious Instruction, where I seemed to bounce from top to bottom. Did well in Arts and Crafts. Highly praised for hard and excellent work as House Captain, in Hockey, athletics, shooting and tennis, which is interesting as I have never had a tennis racquet in my hand!

Obtained 8 "O" levels and went on to 6th form."

Found the work hard but an agreeable pupil who contributed fully to many activities in school.

Needless to say, playing rugby at a young age, introduced me to pints of bitter and many an occasion have I fallen off my cycle, returning from an after-rugby match party and sometimes from a lock in at the Bracknell Working Men's Club. On one such occasion when I had my car (I was born before breathalisers were introduced) I can recall spinning the Fiat on Bracknell High Street and being stopped by a policeman when I was trying to drive into my front drive, having not had the Fiat for very long. He asked me where I lived and I said if he moved to the left I could get in my front drive and that was good enough, I'm pleased to say.

Returning to school matters, apart from athletics, I was fairly involved in school activities generally, I recall appearing in the annual school play in the quadrangle.

On that occasion this was Midsummer Night's Dream and I got the plum job of playing the "wall". All I had to do was to stand around, utter the odd word with my arms outstretched, supporting a canvas with bricks painted on it (already back in the building industry). For perfect visual effect, it was decided that they would distribute some plaster on my head. That was fine but the only way to get it off was to cut my hair in a somewhat patchy manner.

My biggest involvement in extra curricula activities at school was the Cadet Force. We had an Army and an Air Force section so with my dad's background, as soon as I possible could, I joined up for the Army section. I participated fully, travelling in my khaki uniform on the bus every Monday and back home again in the evening. Monday afternoon was the cadet force parade and then lectures, weapon training and so on.

We probably had two or three weekend camps in a year, going to various army locations, often in Aldershot or Hawley Lake near Crowthorne. These weekends involved largely camping but occasionally in barracks and various exercises, assault courses, marches and at Hawley Lake in particular, afloat in canvass assault craft. Needless to say, I managed to get stripes through hard work and was more and more involved in the cadet force. In the end, I was promoted to Company Sergeant Major and then in the last 18 months or so became an Under Officer which is the highest rank that a cadet can obtain and the equivalent of a Second Lieutenant. This privilege allowed me to use the cadet hut, if I wanted to nip away during sixth form lessons for a quiet fag, play at stripping and re-building Bren guns and so on and generally skiving.

In addition to the weekend camps, there were opportunities to go on other courses and I did a guards' drill and weapon training course, became proficient at shooting and we sometimes went to the local Combermere Guards Barracks in Windsor to use their rifle ranges. On other occasions, we also went out to Ash Rangers, again outside Aldershot, which were outside up to a thousand yards shooting ranges. We competed in the annual National Cadet Rifle Championships at Bisley

More particularly, with more involvement in the cadets, I was able to go on a two week trip to the British Army in Germany visiting barracks (and the red light district) in Dusseldorf where if you jay walked across a red light, the police were liable to shoot you in the back of the leg. I also visited Padderbourne which was the headquarters of the fourteenth twenty-first Lancers. They were a tank battalion whose motto was, I recall, 'blood and glory' where I learnt to drive a centurion tank and managed to knock the Commanding Officer off the top of the tank at one point by swinging the turret and he was standing on the top of the tank.

When in Padderbourne we had a visit from the American forces. They had so many vehicle it took hours for them to park up on the parade ground. Elvis Presley was part of the group although we didn't see him!

Also I did a Commando Acquaint Course at Royal Marine Training Headquarters at Lympstone in Devon. I thought I was pretty fit then but I slept for a week when I got home. This was full commando training with twenty-five-mile marches across Dartmoor and then night patrols, sleeping in homemade bivouacs which are tents made with a few sticks and a ground sheet, living off army rations and also carrying out beach assaults from landing craft where I was lucky enough to be given the rope to jump ashore first and hold the boat but as I jumped, the wave went down and the boat went up and I ended up swimming and towing it. They also had the most amazing assault courses, including one where you seemed to crawl for yards and yards and yards through mud, actually it was really swimming and an aerial assault course which I seem to recall was about a mile long, way up in the air and never touching the ground and finishing off with a death slide which was just a strap over a rope from the top of a cliff into the sea. This was great until your rifle swung round from being across your shoulder to placing itself just as you hit the water with the bold of the rifle neatly placed between your legs. I also did some abseiling off the same cliffs. This wasn't the modern abseiling where they seem to have clips and runners, you simply stood astride the rope which was hanging down the cliff, picked it up through between your legs and across your bent elbow which you use as a break and just simply jumped five or ten yards down at a time, at right angles to the cliff. The only problem I had was wearing lightweight jungle green trousers so the friction from the rope missed the trousers and caught my skin.

    A real treat was joining the Eton College Cadets on their summer camp to Loch Ewe in Scotland. Being Eton College of course, it was all done extremely properly and I was fortunate to be in the Officer group as it were. We marched through Windsor to join up with the Eton College contingent at Windsor and Eton Riverside Station where our own train, chartered by Eton College, was ready to take us all the way to Scotland. Everything was provided on the train which probably took twenty odd hours and I know needed a second engine to get up the inclines towards Loch Ewe, probably from Inverness. There was also an NCO's coach which included myself and the other Cadet Officers from Eton and I recall two guards' vans which were liberally loaded with alcoholic drink (and some non-alcoholic) I'm told. One of my fellow privileged passengers, was Prince William of Gloucester who took part in all of the exercises on the summer camp but tragically was killed in 1972 at the age of 30 whilst piloting his own plane in the Goodyear International Air Trophy.

Once we arrived at Loch Ewe, we were prepared for a fairly hectic three weeks, not only in exercises with or even against Eton College but they had arranged to parachute in the Second Battalion on the Parachute Regiment for some exercises against us and also, because it was Eton College, they had arranged for a Norwegian Destroyer to anchor off Lock Ewe and send some hairy Norwegian commandos against us as well. The paras were quite boisterous, shall we say, and more than one cadet who happened to come across the paras at one stage, ended up with a large piece of a branch embedded in his forehead from a swing from a para. You wouldn't have thought they were on an exercise or perhaps they wanted to get their own back against the privileged!

They really were a wild bunch with live ammunition, shooting chickens in the barrack huts and putting holes in the roof etc.

At around that time, I had been keen to join the army as a regular but one hot day (and I still feel the heat) dressed in an army battledress, which was thick and hairy, I decided I couldn't spend the rest of my life in that discomfort and having already got through the preliminary application for Sandhurst Officers' Cadet School, I backed off. After the excursion to Scotland with Eton College, I was invited to the guardroom at the college by the Cadet Commanding Officer, a teacher at the college. I was invited just to have a glass of beer and a general chat and he thanked me sincerely for the great time we had, my considerable contribution to the camp and wished me well. It would have been a nice reference if he'd put it in writing! Nevertheless I was chuffed. I still have my father's old Sam Brown officers belt which I used to wear as an Under Officer. My father's military career was certainly, at some stage, something I thought of emulating. He left the war as a Captain having started as a Private and became Adjutant to the Gloucester Regiment. He was pretty lucky with the war, getting postings teaching at Sandhurst and, for some reason, teaching skiing in Austria! There were other diversions at school with Windsor Girls' School, not too far away and Princess Margaret Rose Girls School just around the corner and walks along the riverside in the evenings were not uncommon but we also used to gather at a coffee bar called The Tartan House, just by the station before we used to go home on buses, at least I did, to Wokingham.

With regard to real school, I used to work hard and conscientiously. I was not top of the class but "tried hard". I think was the more normal report phrase. I did obtain 8 O Levels, I did three A Levels, art, engineering drawing and geography but, as I will explain, I'd got a place at the Regent Street Polytechnic and I was then going out with the daughter of a landlord of a local pub in Binfield. I had an extremely good summer, probably had a bit of a hangover when I took the exams and failed all three. I shared engineering drawing which I recall was taken by two or three of us with a very good friend of mine at school and we are still sort of in touch, Clive Smith who did a little better than me. He was a great golfer and has made a bit of money at golf and indeed owned a couple of golf courses but more particularly, owned Kauto Star which was an extremely successful steeplechase horse, won the Grand National and two other major events in the same year and netted him £4.5m, tax free. If it wasn't for the virus, we were due to have a barbeque at his house on the Wentworth Estate around the lockdown period. It has sort of been penciled in for later in the year.

So what next. As I've said my father was Assistant Secretary at the ICI Jealott's Hill Research Station near Bracknell and was involved in many things, including some of the building works and of course I became involved with the local builders, John C Sargent. I continued to work for them through college, graduating to the office where I got involved in sort of managing contracts and some estimating. After I had left, I was told by Michael Sargent that a job that I had quoted for, I think for a Gas Board house, they'd won but didn't make any money because in measuring the decorations I seemed to have missed out the height of the rooms and one roll of wallpaper wasn't enough! Still, you've got to learn somewhere.

An architect from the North East, linked with when ICI had factories up in the Northumberland area (Billingham I seem to recall) was involved in the major new build at Jealott's Hill and my father dealing with him on a regular basis, they become quite good friends. At the same time, Dad was still organising some smaller works, I recall him sitting at the dining table (with no formal training) drawing up a new milking parlour for the dairy herd. These were all the rage in those days, although by no means anyway near as automated as currently. I showed some interest so he bought home another drawing board and paper etc. and I copied what he was drawing and quite enjoyed it, it wasn't bad. I can't draw a thing these days and I'm certainly not in any way competent in computerised drawings. That's what I employed the lads to do!

Anyway, having shown this interest and it was mentioned to the architect friend (Monty? I seem to recall) and he suggested that we should meet up.

I recall that the then Annual Building Exhibition was held at Olympia – I think it moved later to Earls Court (after the redevelopment of part of that). Monty invited Dad and I up to the exhibition which we toured and then met up in the RIBA lounge for lunch, as Monty's guest

Monty said to me 'so you want to be an architect'? I said yes and he then asked me if I thought I had a design flair, to which I replied 'not really'. Monty then said that 'there is only one Basil Spence! He had just completed Coventry Cathedral, largely destroyed by the wartime bombing and was subsequently the architect for the Knightsbridge Barracks and so on.

Monty, therefore, suggested that I would be best employed (not sure some would agree with that) as a Building Surveyor. So, I duly contacted the RICS and followed that route, in my case, the suggestion that Building Surveyors are generally frustrated architects was about right, although I never felt frustrated about it.

Incidentally, one of the buildings that Monty completed at Jealott's Hill was a modern chemical laboratory block. One evening Dad got a phone call at home to say that the block was on fire, so I went with him to Jealott's Hill and it really was a blaze. This meant a long evening/night on site, helping to get the firemen cups of tea etc. It was subsequently discovered that the fire was what is now known as "spontaneous combustion" with a dry laboratory coat, touching a radiator. Being a chemical laboratory, there were various gas cylinders and one oxyacetylene cylinder exploded and split like a banana. This discharged a toxic cloud, Fosgene, which the fire brigade tracked for a way until it dispersed, somewhere over Maidenhead, I recall.

So, as a Student Member of the RICS (don't think they do that anymore, do they), I managed to apply for and obtain a place at Regent Street Polytechnic (now University of Westminster - although I can't claim a university education). In those days, there weren't university or technical college courses specifically designed for degrees in building surveying, property etc. but we studied for the RICS direct exams. These were set and marked by the RICS and taken at various examination halls around London and the rest of the UK. The Regent Street Polytechnic was a great place to be. It was set up by Quintin Hogg (Lord Hailsham's father). The main building with a large auditorium was, and still is at Upper Regent Street, just above Oxford Circus and convenient to travel to. We were based in the annex in Little Titchfield Street. It housed surveyors, including Quantity Surveyors who shared most of the lectures with ourselves as specialisation only occurred at final exam level, the architects who spent five years mucking about with balsawood and string but more importantly the secretaries, with whom we had a good relationship. There were also a number of pubs in very close proximity, particularly out by the backdoor to the annex and, like all good students, we got to taste the local beers. On a Friday afternoon, we always had a law lecture which was generally given by one or other barrister. Mainly a guy called Simon, who was a young barrister and we generally broke up at tea time and went with him to the pub where he shared some of the juiciest divorce cases he was involved in. Other extra-curricular activities, included visits to brick works, cement works, the occasional building site and land surveying at Kenwood House in Hampstead. That was interesting, with old fashioned theodolites and chains on a piece of land where concerts are performed which has more ups and downs that you can imagine.

I travelled up from Wokingham every day and made some very good and lasting friends although unfortunately a number of the closest friends that I kept in touch with have sadly departed. As I was still playing rugby and the Poly had a rugby team, we used to play at the Polytechnic Sports Ground by Chiswick Bridge and with the relationship with Quintin Hogg, forming the Polytechnic, the team was named 'The Quins'; so I once played for the Quins! Once again, I had too good a time and failed the intermediate exam whilst at the Poly and I don't think my grant would stretch that far so I had to find a job and sign up for the College of Estate Management Correspondence Course, which I think still exists through Reading University.

I did obtain a job and I was very lucky that it was a

good job, with good training. It was also intensive and although I could read my correspondence course papers on the train to and from home, I didn't have any spare time during the week, as I was not only busy but often travelling around the UK working, which I loved. In my first year, I managed to pass the intermediate a second time around and a year later in 1957, passed the final and became a member of the RICS as an Associate and very shortly after, a Fellow of the Royal Institution of Chartered Surveyors in 1975. Whilst I still call myself a Chartered Surveyor, which I can do through my Livery connections in my view, I resigned from the RICS in 2019. I had been running my own practice, as will be seen later, for some considerable time by then but I had moved down from London and with client contacts dying, retiring or outsourcing their business to major practices, I wasn't earning a fortune (but still spending) and I wasn't getting any value for money from the RICS £700 plus per annum. I resigned rather than become a retired member because I wanted to continue practicing (which hopefully once the virus has quietened down), I might still do a bit. I also had great pleasure in telling the Chief Executive of the RICS that I was sorry, having spent, amongst other things, 43 years on and off as a Member of the RICS Governing/General Council. I was fed up with paying a subscription for him to swan around the world, collecting professorships and so on and me getting no benefit.

So, having to leave the Poly in 1963, I was looking for a job and that was not easy at that date. I can't recall which of the five or six property crashes that I've experienced in my career, it was possibly the oil crisis, I think.

I applied directly or through the RICS Appointments Service which existed then, for a number of jobs but I was not particularly successful. I managed to get an interview and was offered a job at Hillier Parker May and Rowden, as they were then. I think it was my eventual employer, Johnnie Johnson, who offered me four-hundred and fifty pounds per year. One of my friends, and indeed we sat next to each other at the Poly, was Norman Cannell and his father who was a Partner at Gardner and Theobald, one of the largest Quantity Surveying firms, suggested I spoke to his friend, Donald Jones, who although qualified as a Quantity Surveyor, was actually running the Building Surveying department at Weatherall Green & Smith (now disappeared) and known as BNP Paribas Estates. I am convinced, because of his friendship with John Cannell, Donald Jones offered me a job at five-hundred pounds per annum which went dramatically up to £1,100 per annum when I passed the final. That was a considerable shock increase and Donald Jones suggested I sat down before he gave me the information.

Weatheralls was a great company and partnership excellent for training. It was well established but still really a family firm with partners whose fathers had been senior partners before them and so on. We had a trainee scheme, although being a building surveyor specialist, we weren't trusted to go and get involved in valuations and property management etc. but in fact the first few months of their time as trainees at Weatheralls was spent in the drawing office so at least they got a little bit of proper training before they went off elsewhere. Indeed, depending on the way the firm moved around, some stayed for a year or more in the drawing office. I was immediately assigned to one of the Senior Surveyors and sat in the drawing office to start with. Being assigned to a surveyor, initially Jimmy Murphy and then subsequently the Associate Dennis Weeks was tremendous because they believed in taking you everywhere with them. So we went on surveys and took the notes (they must have been able read my writing in those days), sat with them in producing their reports and so on. Sometimes they were dictating the reports and certainly Dennis Weeks always insisted that I sat in his office, whilst he was dictating, in those days to a secretary.

I'm afraid that after a year or so, I found this a bit tiresome and thought it was a waste of time and used to go off on my own and do my own things and often Dennis would say to me, how is such and such a job and I would say, just put the fee account in, or, something similar. I was a cocky little sod but believed I knew what I was doing and could get on with it, in a more efficient manner.

I still can't believe now the fees that we charged. Indeed some of them would still look expensive in this day and age. I can recall Dennis saying to a client, who was questioning a fee quote, 'well if you want the best, you've got to pay for it'. Pity we can't get back to those sort of days.

I think the fact is that we were one of very few recognised and experienced Building Surveying teams and relied on specialist departments like the L&G (Legal & General Insurance) who did all of the L&G work at Weatheralls and I don't think another firm advised them. I think there were some other, almost retained clients, such as Shell Petrol and so on. Bear in mind that most major practices were relatively small compared with the current day and major institutions, such as L&G, had fairly small property departments and needed outside advice.

The advantage was that we also had a wide range of contacts and they in turn produced a wide ranging and indeed far ranging list of instructions. As a young Chartered Surveyor (or at least nearly chartered) I enjoyed travelling around the country. I can remember, accompanied by Terry Knight, who subsequently became Senior Partner of Weatherall, Green and Smith, we were charged with carrying out Fire Insurance Valuations on properties owned by Ready Mix Concrete Company. These were all over the UK and many ranged from small sheds and perhaps a gatehouse and weighbridge on a gravel pit or quarry to a few small office buildings and so on. I can remember trudging across in a blizzard to find a small shed on the top of a cliff of the quarry, somewhere in the Midlands and also one of the longest jetties you will ever find at Brightlingsea for loading gravel onto the barges to run up to London. I recall the weather there wasn't very good there either. It was good fun and we used to stay in some reasonable hotels and enjoy expenses.

One job that I wasn't involved in but Dennis Weeks carried out and carried it out over a long period of time, probably up to a year, was the survey of Stowe School. This is a magnificent and large building and I can recall seeing the final report, which was in a number of volumes.

Personally I got involved with Guinness, another

almost retained client and in particular, adjacent to the then existing Guinness Brewery at Park Royal, the industrial estate in Coronation Road, Park Royal, where Guinness owned a load of factories. In particular, Guinness had a fundamental research laboratory organization and we got involved with converting old warehouses and factories into undoubtedly no longer P.C. activities of funding research for the pharmaceutical industry on animals. The quality of work in these research laboratories was of the highest and we did two phases. The second phase was adjacent to the first where the animals were housed and they had not to be disturbed in any way, so we had to devise new ways of breaking up concrete floors. Vibration was not appropriate and in the end, I recall that we ended up cutting with water jets, something which still happens. The joy of working with Guinness, particularly on the brewery that you always had to have meetings up there because they had a pub 'The Toucan Inn' within the brewery complex and everybody working for Guinness there was entitled to take visitors into the pub for a drink at lunchtime.

One of the most fascinating and amazing projects I was involved in with Dennis was the survey of a small, narrow but tall (for Newcastle anyway) office building for an insurance client's, Newcastle base. I don't recall the fee but it was substantial and I think in this day and age, you wouldn't take an assistant and you would probably do the survey and there and back in a day or maximum one night stay over. I recall that the survey was in the winter because we flew up to Newcastle and landed at what was then the RAF base in Newcastle, which I recall acted as the municipal airport as well until Newcastle airport itself was built. Fairly heavy snow on the way into the city. We had been unable to book hotel rooms, we were staying two nights, so headed for the best hotel as always was then, The Station Hotel, then run by British Rail and always excellent. We bowled up to reception saying two rooms for two nights please and they said that they were sorry, they were fully booked. Somewhat aghast, Dennis asked if they could phone around and find us hotels out as far as Gosforth and so on and we went for an excellent dinner. Halfway through dinner, Dennis checked with reception to find that they had one room that had become vacant at, I seem to recall £150 per night for a single, so we took that, enjoyed dinner and a glass of port and low and behold, when we finished dinner, they magically found another such room. It appears, at least in those days, that it was usual to retain at least one or two top rooms in such hotels, should Government Ministers or whatever suddenly appear at very short notice. Strangely enough, although we were only booked for one night, the same rooms became available the next night!

The survey didn't take very long and I can't remember but I guess the building, whilst it was probably five or six floors, quite close to the iconic Newcastle Bridge, was no more than 8-10,000 square feet. Empty, hadn't been occupied for a long time, electrics all old etc., etc. and I've got a feeling in those days that the fee, plus expenses, was somewhere in the region of £10,000. As well as visiting the Local Authority Planning Department etc., etc., we also had an excellent lunch with the client at the Station Hotel and flew back on the third day. That was interesting, we flew there and back on BEA (before British Airways) Elizabethan which was a high wing monoplane with a twin tail fin, a small version of a Constellation, which was a Transatlantic plane.

Fees were good and apart from when were in the office and eating sandwiches or in a little café around the corner off Chancery Lane, we did enjoy the good life. The Partners were all members of the Wig & Pen Club in Fleet Street. Every now and again, we would end up there, if we'd been out with a Partner and I remember on one occasion when Donald Jones and I were in Rotherhithe and got back to Chancery Lane around 3.30/4.00pm, Donald said well the only place for lunch at this time of day is the Wig & Pen where the menu doesn't change between lunch and dinner and is continuous, so we enjoyed that.

Through Donald Jones and more particularly George Vine, who was then Senior Partner, I was introduced to the Worshipful Company of Innholders. George Vine was officially the surveyor to the Innholders Company, although apart from valuation stuff etc., most of the day to day work was done by the building surveyors, with Donald Jones being the main contact.

I did quite a lot of work for the Innholders Company and in particular related to the registration of the Innholders Hall in Little College Street, off Dowgate Hill by Canon Street Station for the Offices, Shops and Roadway Premises Act 1963. I became a bit of an expert in registering toilet and washing facilities and indeed around the same time, also trawled around all of the buildings and Grays Inn, registering them. Grays Inn was a much larger job, being the whole of the Inn's premises off Holborn. I was privileged, having produced a report on what was necessary, to be invited to the Benchers Committee at Grays Inn. The Benchers Committee is the ruling committee of the Inns of Court and I was invited to Grays Inn Hall in Grays Inn Square for, I recall, a 4.00pm meeting to report to the Benchers Committee. As the partner who was the link with Grays Inn wasn't available to report and to be honest didn't understand what I would be reporting anyway, he sent me in his place. The Benchers Committee consist of lawyers and many judges, a number of whom live in the residential properties dotted around the buildings. I duly arrived at the Hall and was told to wait in the library until called. I was duly called upstairs and ushered into the main committee room, I think. In this was the longest polished table I have ever seen and around it, looking at me as I walked through the door, were all of these very distinguished gentlemen and I think one or two ladies. I was summoned to sit by the Chairman who happened to be Lord Edmond-Davies, the judge who carried out the Aberfan disaster enquiry. I made my report and answered questions. I was thanked very much and it was suggested I went back to the library to wait and they would join me shortly.

After a very short wait, they started to come in to the library and it was drinks time. I vividly recall the probably considered notorious Lord Justice Widgery who lived in one of the residential flats, coming in and offering me a drink and I said I would have a whiskey and ice. He put a couple lumps of ice and then almost filled a small tumbler with scotch. It wasn't very long before Widgery approached me again and asked me if I would like the other half!

Following the report, I was then charged with carrying out the necessary works to comply with the Offices, Shops and Railway Premises Act.

A similar result followed from my report on the Innholders Hall. Our contact there was the Beadle, who is basically the up market caretaker who also lived on the premises. At that time, the well-known Beadle who was also a City Toastmaster, was Gordon Marsh. We had I think almost weekly site meetings with the contractor inspecting the works and checking on progress etc., which included fire escape and fire alarm works as well as more mundane items such as providing adequate toilets and so on.

We'd usually start the meeting at 10.30 am or 11.00 am, they didn't take long and on a number of occasions, Gordon Marsh would say to me that they had a dinner in the hall that evening and he thought we ought to test the port, to ensure it was adequate. At the tender age of around 24, I therefore got a taste for port and good port at that and often Gordon and I would end up finishing half a bottle before lunch!

Coincidentally, I've since visited Innholders on a number of occasions, through city functions. As Master Chartered Surveyor, I was privileged since the incoming Lord Mayor, the late Robert Finch, was also a Liveryman of the Chartered Surveyors Company, I along with the City Surveyor, Ted Hartill and Terry Knight were invited to an excellent dinner at Innholders, known as the Presentation Dinner which follows the presentation of the incoming Lord Mayor to the Lord Chancellor as the Queen's representative. Incidentally, we were also very privileged to take a major part in the Lord Mayor's Show, the Silent Ceremony the day before and so on and indeed proceed in the at the Law Courts on the way and lunch in the Mansion House at the end.

Well as usual, I digress. The work at Innholders (which has since been extended by buying the next door property) was fascinating with an Adam ceiling in the Courtroom. This was a heavy moulded ceiling which was in danger of falling to the floor and we arranged for a specialist fibrous company to repair it by wiring up ,with pieces of hessian, plaster and the mouldings up to the floor joists above. It is still there and because of an association with the Past Master Innholder at the same time as I was Master Surveyor, I am told that the fire alarm wiring, which I inserted, is still in very good condition.

Coincidentally again, as a Freeman and Member of the Court of the Company of Waterman and Lightermen of the River Thames, I dine in Innholders Hall once every other year and as we and the Innholders jointly celebrate over 500 years (dependent on which Act you refer to).

I guess working at Innholders and working with Donald Jones, was my first introduction to the City Livery movement which in latter years took a very large part of my life, both socially and from the Livery movement, as well as introductions for business. In fact, I did work out at one stage that after being made redundant from Hillier Parker and starting up my own practice, whether first, second or third hand referrals, 50% of my business was linked to the Livery movement.

Donald Jones was a Liveryman of the Worshipful Company of Painter Stainers and indeed a member of the Painters Lodge. I was proposed by Donald Jones and seconded by a boating friend who was a contractor in the City, became a Freeman of the City of London and a Liveryman of the Painter Stainers Company. The Painter Stainers was, to a certain extent, construction orientated, with many liverymen being in the construction industry or surveyors and in particular quantity surveyors. Unfortunately, I had to resign following redundancy from Goodman Price, a demolition company as described later and it was a while before I got back into the livery movement.

Donald Jones was also responsible for introducing me to the RICS.

Weatheralls were an RICS supporting company with staff and partners playing a full role on the Central London Branch of the RICS, as well as the auctioneers and estate agents committee and also in my initial involvement, the Junior organisation of both organisations before they became merged into the RICS.

I think my first involvement was on the London Juniors Committee of the RICS and indeed, the National Junior Organisation, both of which eventually led to me becoming a member of both the Hermes Club (ex London Juniors) and the 1913 Club (National JO) where I am still a member. The RICS is renowned for dining clubs, although they seem to be dying out a bit now and there again were great stepping stones and social organisations. As a buliding surveyor, I was very much in the minority on these organisations, although I did eventually become Chairman of both the Hermes and the 1913 Club and dining with the general practitioners allowed me to make some very good and long standing friends and indeed clients. This involvement in the RICS continued through all levels for over 50 years, culminating in being elected as President of the RICS Building Surveyors Division when Divisions existed and before their sad dissolution.

Donald Jones started life as a Quantity Surveyor but then worked as a Building Surveyor and ran the Building Surveying department. He was a Building Surveying champion and as I worked for him at the time, I can vouch for the fact that he was instrumental in the formation of the Building Surveyors Division. As I have said, this is now no longer, although there is still a surviving dinner for Past Presidents and Chairmen who took over the role after the dissolution of the divisions and I have pleasure to be organising that dinner at the end of the Coronavirus lockdown, hopefully. It is now entitled The Donald Ensom Dinner, as Donald Ensom was the first President. As I say, Donald Jones was instrumental in forming the division because I know that he spent probably two years going through the RICS membership book and directory and checking against exam results, to prove that at that point there were more than 1500 who had qualified in the old iii(b) final exam syllabus, which was a Building Surveying speciality. The Donalds persuaded the RICS General Council, as it was then, that there should be a Building Surveying Division. I recall that then there was only the General Practice and Quantity Surveying Divisions, so we became the third division at the time. Donald Jones was the first Chairman of the new division and Donald Ensom the first President in 1973-1976 and I followed in 1993/94. I was also Chairman of the Central London Branch of the RICS in 1990/91, again following Donald Jones.

The Division having been formed, I suggested through the then Chairman of the Central London Branch Committee, one Eric Real of Drivers Jonas, that there should be a Central London Building Surveying Committee, to which he agreed and suggested that since I could write letters, I should be the first secretary. I subsequently chaired that committee. For the next 43 years, on and off, I served on Governing and General Council, the Management Board which was the President's Management Committee, the RICS Education Trust and amongst many other things, became the Consultant Building Surveyor to Great George Street. Incidentally I also, in my demolition days, dealt with the partial demolition in 1979 for the refurbishment and alteration extension at the rear of Great George Street and again, coincidentally, sat on the Redevelopment Committee for the complete refurbishment of the whole building internally in the 2000's.

So, my years at Weatherall Green and Smith was not only an extremely good start to professional life but it gave me an introduction to excellent clients and the Livery movement in the City and the Royal Institution of Chartered Surveyors. It certainly got me interested in socialising, both on committees, at the Three Tuns on

Chancery Lane on a Friday evening and so on. Unfortunately as I write this, in the middle of the Coronavirus lockdown and in recent years because of being a sole practitioner, without a very good expense account, I've got out of the habit of some of these but fortunately the Livery movement and in particular the Watermen's Company have managed to keep me in touch. My time at Weatheralls ended on a fairly friendly basis but I felt that my way to future promotion was slightly blocked by Dennis Weeks who was an Associate and I was told wouldn't ever make a Partner and therefore was in my way. Indeed, he did eventually become an Equity Partner and also my successor, Paul Gardner was also made an EP later on in life.

I therefore decided to look for pastures new and happened to come across Michael Brooks who had just broken away as the building surveying team of an Estate Agents in Kensington to start his own practice with the now late Nicholas Goodwin, who sadly died. I came in to fill the gap left by Nicholas and joined Michael as a Partner, working with him from 1971 to 1974. We built up the practice, Michael was particularly strong in party wall matters so I became a party wall expert as well, something which I still carry out under the later 1996 Act but I also building up project management and construction supervision work on the contract side.

We were very fortunate that Michael, who had also been in practice with another guy in the Kensington practice, who went on to become Managing Director of Trafalgar House Properties and we did an awful lot of development work for Nigel Brokes and Trafalgar House on major city developments. We operated from a mews property in Adam & Eve Mews, which was convenient because if also had parking on the ground floor and as I always did subsequently, we both used cars a lot, even around Kensington, Chelsea, Knightsbridge etc.. I guess traffic was probably a bit lighter but it was much easier to get from one to the other and see more sites than flogging on tubes, buses and walking. One of the properties that I was involved in was No 1 Orme Square. This was purchased by Prince Jah of Hyderabad. The Prince's mother still lived at the time in a massive house in Kensington Park Gardens where I had some involvement in bits and pieces. Orme Square was off Bayswater and the Prince purchased the property next door to Jeremy Thorpe and his lovely wife, both of whom I met on a couple of occasions.

When I first met Prince Jah, as is my want, I asked him his background and whilst I knew that India was part of the Commonwealth, I wasn't, quite sure where Hyderabad fitted in. He told me quite simply that Hyderabad was in fact 'nationalised'. His father was then the Nizam of Hyderabad. It was sure some nationalisation as the ruling family came away with substantial holdings and I know that Prince Jah himself had properties in Turkey and Hyderabad and London and Ireland at least, as well as asbestos factories in Hyderabad and so on. When I first met him and the Princess, who was utterly charming, they lived in a ground floor flat in a modern block of flats developed by again, coincidentally, Trafalgar House. Indeed, Nigel Brokes who formed Trafalgar House lived in a detached property at the rear of the development, which had formed I guess a small spin off for Nigel Brokes for his own personal use. During the work at No 1 Orme Square, I used to meet the Prince and Princess, I seem to recall on a Thursday morning and I always had luch with them in their flat, although I forewent the Turkish coffee, a taste which I have still not acquired, even having an apartment in the Turkish part of Cyprus. Again coincidentally, I got involved in a party wall matter when the block of flats was adjoined by another development and the top floor penthouse was occupied by the then Chairman of Cunard Shipping, which again coincidentally was taken over by Trafalgar House.

Whilst at Michael Brooks Associates, we took on a number of assistants, one of whom was ex Weatherall Green a long time ago, as indeed was Michael Brooks, coincidentally again, also I took on Alex Schatunowski straight from Loughborough College as a graduate. Not the only reason for taking him on, but his mother lived in Caversham as well so he was quite a useful chauffeur home after a good lunch! Another and still a great friend of Alex's by the name of Ed Keelahan eventually become a Senior Partner of a building surveying specialists, Hunter and Partners who were also based in Kensington at the time.

One project I was working on at Michael Brooks was a house in Montpelier Square. This was a refurb of the whole house for the Honorable Robert Cecil who was shortly going to get married. Robert is now the current Lord Salisbury and again a coincidence, I met him at the Waterman's Hall when he was giving a lunchtime talk following the Queen's Diamond Jubilee River Pageant which he organised and we took part in out boat.

As part of the work on the Montpelier Square house, we had to serve Party Structure Notices on Adjoining Owners, one of whom was represented by Bryan Anstey whom I met on site to agree the party structure matters. Bryan Anstey's name is synonymous with rights of light, as he was the author of the original book on rights of light and rights of light matters and indeed his son, the late John Anstey was a leading light in the formation of the Pyramus and Thisby Club, which was a party wall surveyors' club which I was involved in at its formation. On site at Montpelier Square, Bryan was a charming person and I had quite an interesting chat about various things including rights of light of which I knew very little (and don't know much more now). When I got back to the office, I spoke to Alex Schatunowski and asked him, as a graduate, if he was interested in rights of light, he knew nothing, but said he would be, and I therefore dispatched him down to the RICS library to get hold of a copy of Bryan Anstey's book which he did and read and learnt. Within a couple of days, he was drawing the Waldram diagrams by which the areas and compensation values of loss of light are calculated. He became and still is one of the principal rights of light experts in the country, now semi-retired ,having sold out to GVA Grimley. I have mentioned the Pyramus and Thisby Club and that I was involved at the beginning and in fact, I think I can consider myself one of three founder members. John Anstey phoned the aforementioned Donald Ensom as to whether it might be worth forming a

Party Wall Surveyors Club of some sort. Donald with whom I served on various RICS Committees phoned me and in consultation with Michael Brooks, I said yes, a good idea and therefore the Pyramus and Thisby Club was formed and is still going. It was in fact instrumental in getting an update that the old 1939 London Building (Amendment) Act which set down the party wall regulations. Another member of the Pyramus and Thisby Club, Lord Johnny Lytton, was the man that got it through the Lords in 1996.

Whilst at Michael Brooks, I was introduced to a client, one Paul Hatfield. We got on well and I'm not sure we actually did a lot in terms of client work, we just talked about a lot of schemes. BY then, as referred to later on, I was already interested in boating and had my own boat and was fairly well involved in the Thames. Paul suggested that he was interested in buying a boat and I knew one that was on the market and I thought would suit him, he looked at it with myself and he decided to buy it. He was then abroad and I was asked to suggest the name which out of the blue I suggested 'Hatters'. When he discovered it, Paul was delighted as Hatters was his nickname. Paul subsequently got big ideas and looked at a Weymouth 50 foot to be built to his specification but for reasons that will become obvious shortly, that didn't happen.

After a long drawn out negotiation and legal documents, Paul, much to his surprise actually, eventually concluded the purchase of Goodman Price Demolition. Goodman Price was one of the largest, longest established and best known demolition companies. They had been involved in the demolition of buildings, subsequently replaced by Broadcasting House, the Savoy, the Stock Exchange and when I joined, were in the process of demolishing the Old London Bridge. Therefore, when the purchase was agreed, Paul offered me the job of Managing Director. I was on a year's notice with Michael Brooks, which Michael insisted I maintained.

I was tempted with a fantastic salary, a company Mercedes and so on and a fairly expansive lifestyle which Paul enjoyed and believed in.

Being cautious, I had an accountant look at the company accounts and there was £500k in cash in the bank, there was a reasonable amount of work on the books, I checked the proposed contract with lawyers and that got the green light so I went ahead.

As I've said, I think it went on so long that Paul, who was a bit of a showman to say the least, could also be called a little bit flash! He went on a spending spree around the world, then experienced another recession, I'm not sure which one it was but it was around 1975 ish and as MD, I noticed with declining workloads that we had a cash flow problem. My initial reaction was to ask for the £500k, guess what? It was leant to finance company A in the Channel Islands which in turn lent it to finance company B which is turn purchased the shares of Goodman Price with it. That meant that the company bought its own shares. This was a Section 54 of the Companies Act Violation which was organised by two of the biggest and best lawyers in the City, Goodwin Derek, for whom Ralph Goodman's son worked and Herbert

Smith. It's fine as a deal if you don't need the money to run the company. I cancelled Paul's American Express card whilst he was away and left him partially stranded in New Zealand. I started to look for a job and a car.

My time at Goodman Price was short but interesting. I got involved in measuring and quoting large contracts including the Whitbread Brewery site in Chiswell Street. I learnt about scrap values, high value non-ferrous metals in gas works and so on.

My joint MD was Ralph Goodman who became Master of the Paviours Livery Company, so we were introduced to the Livery movement and a white tie Banquet at the Mansion House. That to be followed by quite a few more over the Years.

Goodman Price also financed my first entertaining 50 guests a day on the boat (and a Marque) at Henley Regatta. This continued for many years for a variety of clients and contractors including John Lelliott and Costains whose PR man was John Rice, Anneka's father, I discovered years later.

Ostensibly as a business generating visit, I called in my old mate from the RICS Central London Building Surveyors Committee, Vic (Johnny) Johnson at Hillier Parker to see if they had any demolition work required. As always, with discussions with Johnny, we ranged across everything but that and he said that he was looking for a successor. We parted and I said nothing for a week and Johnny subsequently said he had never known me keep that quiet for that long. I telephoned him and said that if he was looking for more than a successor, I could be interested. In a very short space of time I then had an interview with the then Senior Partner of Hillier Parker, Len Jarrard, again someone whom I worked with and known from RICS Central London Branch and other connections. I was subsequently offered a job and this time I accepted and became an Associate and eventually in 1983 became an Equity Partner No 21 in the list in those days. Coming in to the department, as it were, over the top of everybody with one or two long servers who might have thought they could take over, I was I think viewed with a little suspicion but my number two, the late Ian Major and I had gone through college together so that made life fairly easy and a couple of the old stagers decided to find pastures new. I eventually became the seventh Senior Partner with 40 staff and within an amazing turnover from the Building Surveying Department in 1979/80 of £3m we did well through the 79/80 downturn and continued for quite a while, making a profit whilst the rest of the firm, particularly the Investment Department wasn't. That was all subsequently forgotten when I was made redundant in 1996, as I refused to make some of my team redundant. That was somewhat amusing as it was clear in meetings with the then Chairman, Donald Newell and Managing Director, Rod Grant that they had no idea what we did. They wanted the Architects Department (which didn't exist we had an architect only) closed and didn't realise how much of the income was actually generated by having the architect and able to sell architectural services, although all of the work was done by draughtsmen or surveyors. They quoted Steve Armitage as the highest earner, which in fact he was and he was doing major refurbishment projects but he wasn't actually doing them all, he had draughtsmen and the architect, Mike Turner, was working on his schemes as well. There we are, despite making a profit, they wanted us to increase out income and although the Management Department, for whom we had some 800 files current, would only pay £50 per hour, the Partners wanted £100 per hour from everybody including the draughtsmen!

So it was decided that as I refused to make Mike Turner and others redundant they got rid of me instead. A few months before that my nomination as a potential candidate in an election for the RICS President (backed by all other Divisional Presidents) was accepted. Subsequently Don Newell suggested that I withdrew that, at which point I said 'you are clearing the decks to get rid of me' which of course happened a few months later.

At Hillier Parker, during my 10 years as Associate/Partner in charge, we grew the department, appointed some Associates and got involved with some large scale projects, some generated by us but most for clients of other departments, particularly on the project monitoring side and project management. On the project monitoring side certainly acting on the development of Embankment Place, the curved building over Charing Cross station was one that one deals with once in a lifetime. We acted for I recall 22 funding banks with the lead bank being the Bank of Tokyo.

Early on I decided that we needed an architect on the team, not only to do the work but more particularly to draw in that side of the work that building surveyors could then do. Len Jarrard advised me that Mike Turner, who had been the lead architect for Peterborough Council and the Queensgate Shopping Centre in Peterborough had virtually finished the contract so I went up and met Mike Turner on the pretext of being given a guided tour of the Centre and offered him a job and he came to London and worked through until retirement and unfortunately a few years later he passed away. A great architect and a great character and great friend. Mike's presence also encouraged project monitoring work as well as architectural/supervision work and would often be involved in initial client interviews to add to the building surveying expertise. With regard to monitoring shopping centre development, the largest one was probably the Charles Darwin Centre in Shrewsbury which was really in place of three other adjacent shopping centres, running down to the river. It was a large centre, although not necessarily the largest (I think Redditch was around one million square feet including the car parks, which I dealt with the final phase of). The Charles Darwin Centre was monitored on behalf of Royal Assurance who subsequently became Royal Sun Alliance and for that same client, monitored the construction of the Sovereign Shopping Centre in Weston Super Mare. This was a fairly long, drawn out job, taking six years overall if I recall because the Local Authority hadn't thought to mention that there was a large restrictive covenant over the ground adjacent and left the Royal to sort that out. When I was first involved, the plan was to build around an existing multi-storey car park but over a weekend I inspected the car park and some engineering reports of concrete corrosion to the structure and recommended that whilst this could be rectified, you would always have an old car park in the middle of a new development!

The Charles Darwin Centre, involved regular monthly meetings with developer and team and again the Charles Darwin Centre was delayed because of another suddenly discovered restrictive covenant which took another two and a half years to sort out before we started. That was interesting because being built on the side of the river, the structure needed piling and the piling rig needed to be so long that it had to be in two sections and built on site. Again through Mike Turner's influence and indeed a considerable influence because he in fact did a lot of the brand design again for Royal Insurance, we secured the project management and indeed construction supervision of the refurbishment of the Eastgate Centre in Inverness. This has since been extended considerably but the work we did was extensive and successful. Mike Turner came up with the logo which was actually a Celtic knot. By that time, we had exported building surveyors from London to the Edinburgh Hillier Parker office, led by Jim Wright who actually was a Scot, returning to his homeland although his family home was Newton Stewart which is not that easy to get to from Edinburgh. A fact I discovered in the monitoring that I was doing for the completion of a shopping centre in Airdrie, following a survey and some defects that I noted where in fact problems with the contractor and developer occurred, that I think I eventually made something like 70 odd visits to sort this one out. For one early morning drains test, I suggested that Jim could help me and he could go home to the family in Newton Stewart at our expense and join me on Monday. What I didn't realise was that rail services etc. from Newton Stewart are not that great and he had to leave on Sunday to meet me at 9.00am on site in Airdrie on Monday. Nevertheless, Jim and Steve Allen (his number two in Edinburgh) got deeply involved in the Inverness project with me travelling up once a month for a major site meeting with the client and contractor etc. We had a Clerk of Works employed but again travelling wasn't that easy and in those days it was a flight from Gatwick on Dan-Air. Subsequently I think becoming British Caledonian and going bust. Because of the travelling time, it wasn't possible to arrive on site until latish morning so time for a progress walk around before a quick beer and part of the site meeting in the afternoon followed by marketing meetings etc. on the second morning, flying back in the afternoon to Gatwick.

This therefore necessitated an overnight stay for everybody with sometimes Mike Turner also coming up from London, the client coming up from London, Jim and Steve from Edinburgh, the mechanical engineer from London and so on. To try to reduce costs, we found a small hotel within 10 minutes walking distance. This was amazing and in the days of North Sea oil, we discovered the portions were gargantuan. The hotel was a converted large Inverness house with extensions to the rear, forming a bit of a rabbit warren. There was one room at the rear which was almost literally a broom cupboard and it was part of the game checking in on the first day that we suggested somebody who could either take a joke or who was a nuisance should have that room. As I say, portions were rally gargantuan and we never actually found a reasonable sized dish. They had on the menu and when I asked to see it, they did have them there and then, 20 ounce Porterhouse Steaks. Trying to find a small portion I ordered Scampi and counted 40 of them, Roast Duck drooped off the end of an oval plate and so on. If you wanted an omelet for breakfast, it was at least a dozen eggs!

You can imagine that with about 8/10 of us it was an amusing evening and it got to the point where the hotel said they were closing the bar but we could go and help ourselves as long as we wrote down what we had!

On one occasion when I was Building Surveying President and had to get back to London for a Council Meeting on a Tuesday, I decided to get up early on my own and fly back on the second day which would have been everybody else's first day. I was at a boat club reception on the Sunday lunchtime and was told that it was blowing a hooley in Scotland (it was I think a week after the tanker the *Brear* had foundered). I telephoned BA who said the flight was ongoing for a Sunday evening and duly flew up to meet the clerk of works with some fairly heavy snow having fallen. Obviously I had an overnight bag and I'd taken the precaution of packing a hip flask, just in case. Next morning the guys from London were stuck as Inverness Airport was closed and they didn't get up, including Mike Turner who had a lot of presentation boards for a presentation to all of the retail tenants. Steve and Jim were stopped at the snow gate on the A8. I therefore made the presentation without the presentation boards, to be told by the clerk of works that he didn't realise that I knew anything about the scheme! Come mid-afternoon we were advised that the airport would be closed and no flights that night, Jim Wright and Steve actually made it by 5/6 pm by which time I had booked on the evening sleeper to London. This is one of those train journeys that I'm sure Michael Portillo would be happy to run as a great railway journey!

As Jim and Steve arrived, we had a quick briefing in the Station Arms and I duly got on the train. Fortunately as the presentation meeting was not attended by all who could have been there, including some retail tenants, there had been a lot of refreshments left over so I scooped up sandwiches and sausage rolls and put them in my overnight bag. That was fortunate as things turned out because there was a buffet car but it was literally that, with burgers and bits and pieces and not much else. I think we pulled out at about 8.00 in the evening and I therefore adjourned to the buffet car, had a couple of beers and a burger or something and I was still sitting there at midnight when the train stopped at Aviemore and some ski fanatics got on. I decided it was time to turn in! As I was in first class and a sleeper I had told the attendant that I wanted to be woken at 6.00am ready to get off in London. At about that time I woke and looked out of the window to see snow, went to the attendant and asked if we were still in Scotland, to which the answer was yes but we're getting closer to the border sir. He asked me if I'd like my early morning tea as ordered and I say yes. He arrived with a tray and a teapot etc. which I put on the bunk then promptly went to get my old brick mobile phone, knocked over the hip flask which poured whisky over my clean shirt, then sat back on the bed and bounced the tea up and the tea (very hot) severely bit me in the bum and I had to spend the rest of the journey, which was some hours, on a tea soaked bunk. Ended up in London 17 hours after the train left Inverness and I was rather glad that I'd nicked the refreshments from the presentation.

During my period at Hillier Parker, I became the Building Surveying Divisional President of the RICS and as I've mentioned previously was proposed but subsequently withdrawn as a candidate for the RICS Presidency.

I had a great time as Building Surveying President. I toured all of the UK branches and Hong Kong and Singapore where in five days, I made 22 presentations and speeches to Hong Kong polytechnics, universities, dinners etc. and travelled to Singapore with my wife in tow. I also made a couple of presentations in New Zealand on behalf of Clive Lewis, who was then the RICS President who discovered I was going there on holiday to visit my wife's cousins in Auckland and asked me if I could do a couple of speeches for him, which I did.

Hillier Parker were at that time worried about the representation on Livery Companies with Richard Ellis and Jones Lang making all the running and Donald Newell suggested that we needed to go forward. I was considered because of my RICS work and indeed said it made sense because I was already a Freeman of the City and Liveryman of the Painter Stainers Company so I was half way there. I therefore went forward and joined the

Worshipful Company of Chartered Surveyors in 1990 and was elected to the Court in 1998, just a couple of years after I was made redundant as a Partner at Hillier Parker so Hillier Parker had never had, to my knowledge, an RICS Divisional President and won't because there aren't any more and hasn't had a Master of the Worshipful Company of Surveyors either so there I was, redundant again and looking for a job and a car.

I was redundant at the age of 55 but I did have a good six months of gardening leave which wasn't gardening because I carried on working, paid at Hillier Parker, entertaining every single contact I could think of at Hillier Parker's expense. On one such occasion I was eating at the RAC Club with my top contact at Royal Mail when somebody I knew, actually through shooting, was Geoffrey Reid of Geoffrey Reid Associates, Architects who had fairly recently escaped the clutches of advertising mogul Martin Sorrell. Geoff Reid when he saw me at the RAC knew I was unemployed, asked me to see him and by the time I got back to the office he had phoned, fixed a meeting and I met him. He said he always wanted a building surveying section in the architectural practice so I became Reid Lamden working in their offices. I was able to walk from Hillier Parker on a Friday to Geoffrey Reid's offices in Portland Place on a Monday with Susie, with a computer, desk and accountancy team etc. Unfortunately, however, whilst I carried on building surveying contacts and making a bit of money, the connection with Geoffrey Reid didn't really work because architects don't think that anybody needs to manage jobs other than them and they don't need project managers so they weren't very good at promoting us to clients, many of whom were top notch so initially, still in their offices and then moving to Hanover Street, we became Brian Lamden Associates.

During this time, albeit a one man band but still thanks to Christies amongst others, earning a reasonable income, I became Master of the Worshipful Company of Chartered Surveyors in 2005/6. This was a magnificent year and I made the most of it with 150 different functions, both hosting and as a guest. We organised a long weekend in Barcelona for 28 Liverymen and their partners which was a great success in no small way due to all of the work that Dee did behind the scenes. We visited La Sagrada Familia. I think that's the last time that the Company has had a weekend away, certainly abroad. Obviously being on the circuit as well as organizing our own functions, we visited many Livery Halls. The Company doesn't have its own hall so we were peripatetic. As Master and with my boating background, I decided that the year would be based on a nautical theme but also taking into account my Livery initial involvement at the Company of Painter Stainers which was really my mother company. We therefore visited and had lunches or dinners at Trinity House, on Head Quarter Ship Wellington, the Headquarters of the Master Mariners' Company, Painter Stainers Hall and so on.

The highlight as Master was undoubtedly the first for a long time and I'm not sure that has been once since. A Company Banquet at the Mansion House. Again, thanks to Dee's help, we prevailed upon 53 of our local friends, boating friends and so on to make up a total full house of

320 at the Mansion House Dinner. As well as the Lord Mayor, Sir David Brewer and Lady Mayoress Tessa, we also had the band of the Blues and Royals and State Trumpeters. An awe inspiring and wonderful event which is still being talked about by our local friends, particularly as they learnt, and practiced in their kitchens, the Loving Cup Ceremony.

We were very lucky that year with Sir David Brewer, as he became, as Lord Mayor with his lovely lady Tessa whom we've met on a number of occasions since. David is President of our Past Masters Association of that year. On retiring as Lord Mayor, he became Lord Lieutenant of London which is the Queen's representative and then was installed by Her Majesty as a Knight of the Ancient Order of the Garter. To my knowledge he is the only retiring Lord Mayor to be so honoured.

During that year there were actually seven Chartered Surveyors who were Masters of Livery Companies and I was able to organise a private lunch for us all with the Lord Mayor in the private dining room at the Mansion House.

One other highlight was a visit and reception on HMS Albion which was the second largest ship in the Royal Navy. She was anchored at Greenwich and we were invited to celebrate on board the 250th Anniversary of the Sea Cadets, together with the Seamens' Society if I recall. The Queen arrived by helicopter and proceeded below decks to what was basically the hanger for the commando carrier where various demonstrations took place and where the reception was held. The Queen was guided around the hanger in various directions and at one point was opposite us and I noticed the Admiral in charge looking around and directing her in my direction. Delighted to say that with a glass of wine in my left had behind my back, she came over and shook my hand and asked me, "What is that badge you are wearing?" I replied, "The Master of the Worshipful Company of Chartered Surveyors your Majesty." She said, 'Chartered surveyors?' and I replied, "Yes, Ma'am, you are our patron and there are a lot of us about, even more than there are chartered accountants." I think that's true or it was true then!

Also we attended another garden party at Buck House, having attended the first one with Clive Lewis when I was Building Surveyor Division President. It's a great honour to be there but also to be honest a bit of a bun fight! You are invited to tea and that together with scones and cakes is all you get. If you want coffee you can't have it.

At the Worshipful Company of Chartered Surveyors you leave the Court five years after passing through the chair and I had such a great year that I decided that I would like to continue with the Livery involvement. The Company had, for some time, had an office in the Hall of the Company of Watermen and Lightermen of the River Thames and I had on a number of occasions helped entertain, prior to dinner, the then Master of the Watermens' Company and the Clerk so I got to know them and also because of my boating connections knew a number of the Freemen of the Watermens' Company. I therefore asked if they would take me in and was welcomed, well almost with open arms I think and became a Freeman of the Watermens' Company (no Livery, a long story but they are a City company without Livery–not because they are ruffians and scoundrels which is why I joined them! but because of the Act of Parliament by which they set up).

Watermens' Hall is a small but lovely hall consisting of three terraced properties joined together over various years with one of the three being a listed Ancient Monument, No 43 in the list of ancient monuments with the other buildings being Grade I also. The ancient monument building is actually the only surviving Georgian Livery Hall.

Once a Freeman of the Company I was fully involved in all of their functions and it wasn't too long before I was seconded to a Development Committee because of my property knowledge and then made an Honorary Court Assistant for three years currently renewed for another three years. For a year I spent a lot of time for no fee involved on the Development Committee. The committee was formed to look at the building an in particular the upper two floors to improve the Company's income from those two floors. The two floors consisted of a master flat which is currently let on the market with a small office suite and other small residential suites. We produced schemes for improving the accommodation with rental values from Savills and put a report forward. I must confess that when I joined the Development Committee, I was naïve in assuming that funds were available but when the report was read, the Company and the Finance and General Purposes Committee in particular said it was excellent but now we need to find the money! That came as a shock to me so I had basically wasted a year of my time although I enjoyed it and because of my stint on the Development Committee in that particular year, I was invited to various other functions within out and outside the Company, in effect as a Chairman of a Committee which happened every year but only once for me including lunch with the Lord Mayor of Westminster in his eyrie then in City Hall, Victoria Street. I am still actively involved in the Company which is at the moment temporarily closed down like the rest of England for the virus but it's a great Company and I've made many, many super friends and enjoyed some great functions. Watermans Company never seems to run out of alcohol at any function but I have learnt my lesson and tend now not to join in the stirrup cup and more importantly the Walrus and the Carpenter pub up the road, especially when there are Past Masters around. I am still suffering from a dislocated shoulder from one such adventure.

In my 24 years or so practicing on my account almost entirely as a one man band I was working in the West End until 2017 and then as clients died or outsourced to larger companies etc., I moved and worked from home where I am currently although still trying hard to generate business not exceeding too well but one or two old contacts still come back from time to time.

In that period since Hillier Parker in a variety of guises and joint ventures with a large part of the time working on my own I have managed to attract a variety of instructions and indeed even when I was Master of the Worshipful Company of Chartered Surveyors in 2005/6, as a one man band with Susie I still managed to bill £150k per annum which wasn't bad! Unfortunately in the last few years, income has dropped considerably to strictly making a loss in the company although still paying some income tax! I have been living for a couple of years on my pension but unfortunately that was converted to a SIPP when I left Hillier Parker (I'm not sure whether that was the right move or not but I was advised accordingly) and my SIPP is reducing quite rapidly with my pension fund drawings that at the moment I shall be reduced to a couple of small annuities and the State Pension only to live on in 8 years. It has to be said that at the moment I still have my boat and an apartment in Cyprus which I hope after the lockdown to be able to get to visit again. Trying to save money to stretch the SIPP a bit but not wanting to live a pauper's life until I have to. On my own I was quite lucky to continue some of my Hillier Parker contacts and also make some new ones but generally new ones via old ones and Livery connections etc. In the good years I did a lot of work for Christies Auction House with refurbishing one building, redecorating externally twice, installing a new transformer in the building and so on. Like all of these things unfortunately they don't last forever, particularly when the Director in charge of property is moved to Global Finance and you can't get close to the person who takes over.

 Currently just talking again to a long standing client, the Westminster Almshouses Foundation and after a break and with a change of personnel and secretary etc., I shall be doing some work for them shortly. I was also a Consultant Building Surveyor to the RICS Headquarters.

That was largely when Hillier Parker who I think still might be, through CBRE, surveyors to the RICS. One of the sad losses where I was doing a lot of work until relatively recently was the Greater Manchester Pension Fund who out sourced their property work to JLL. I did a lot of refurbishment, quite regular acquisition surveys, dilapidations and so on. Outsourced to La Salle Investment Management I knew a couple of Directors there and met them and asked of the outsourcing. They told me that they don't give everything to JLL, well they do!

One thread that I've hardly mentioned but has been a large part of our life for the 54 years of marriage and indeed a little before that in my case is boating.

During my time of studies at Regent Street Poly, I sat next to and got very friendly with Norman Cannell. In fact we subsequently married sisters and were each other's respect Best Men. He could afford to get divorced but I'm still married! When we first started at college, Norman's father, John Cannell then Senior Partner of Gardiner & Theobald who originally introduced me to Weatherall Green & Smith, had a small 28 foot plywood boat called Kynance. Very shortly after her, however, John purchased a much larger vessel by the name of Doutelle and during the boating season, Norman and I commandeered the boat at weekends, holidays etc., entertaining a string of lady friends, some of whom joined for one night of the weekend only. Norman's father was a member of the Upper Thames Motor Yacht Club and the club was sort of based, unofficially at Busnells Boat Yard at Wargrave and Doutelle actually moored there as well. Therefore the UTMYC figures large in my life. Joining as an Associate in 1965 and a full member when we purchased our first boat in 1968. We were very active in the Club in those days, boat handing competitions were very popular although they seem to almost totally died out now. Norman and I competed in every one we could and between us on Doutelle and then subsequently on our own boats, we won many trophies. I was made a member of the Upper Thames Committee as an Associate and indeed presented with a trophy for the person who contributed most to the Club in that period. During our dual use of the boat obviously I met Dee and we then enjoyed weekends with Norman's girlfriend and subsequent wife, Dee's sister Daphne. It had been discovered a while before, not when the boat was purchased that Doutelle was in fact a Dunkirk boat and in 1963, before the discovery was confirmed, the Evening Standard ran a Jubilee Pageant on the river and invited six boats that they had discovered were Dunkirk boats although this was the first notice that the owners had, as the original plaques handed to them after Dunkirk had been taken with the old owners. We sailed past the Queen who took the salute on the steps of the old County Hall, as it was then and ended up moored at Putney Pier with the owners and passengers of the six, now newly recognised Dunkirk little ships sitting, in deck chairs under the street lamps having a drink or two. It was suggested at that point that there should be formed a Dunkirk Little Ships Association which subsequently had a meeting the following year at the Little Ships Club and the Association of Dunkirk little ships was formed. In the first six boats, the first Commodore was Commander Charles Lamb who had a wooden leg and a sailing boat. He was a complete rogue and great fun and had during the war flown a Swordfish and I think was involved in torpedoing the Bismark. He wrote a book called War in a String Bag which is fascinating. Also there was Raymond Baxter. Another lovely man and a bit of a rogue and the third member, a large bearded man by the name of John Knight who had a wonderful sense of humour and a great laugh and earned money by boiling and packing beetroot for Tesco's and did very well at it.

The Association was formed and I became the first Treasurer, I think ,which in this day and age seems strange because I can never understand accounts. I've never actually managed to do a return at one of the Dunkirk reunions but there is still time when they re-start next year. I got involved with the Association from the beginning although drifting away more after I got my own boat and was more and more involved in the Upper Thames. Indeed the Upper Thames has a lot to answer for since slightly indirectly Denise and I met through the Club and it's been a large part of our married life of 54 years.

In fact when we got married, as we were already involved in the boating scene, looking for somewhere to live, we started at Hurst Park where they had houses but were too expensive at £5,000 and worked out way up river until we got to Caversham Park Village outside Reading and found a house for £500 less. We've lived in that area ever since and close to the river and at this moment in time still use the river, walking the dog and just being close by and using restaurants there etc. and boating.

Less than six months after we got married we actually purchased our first boat which was a boat called Fruna which was a Freeman 22 which is still going and moored, last time I saw, down in Sunbury and we paid £1,500 for it and if I recall sold it for £2,000. We then purchased a second hand 27 foot Elysian aft cockpit boat with a single diesel engine and that did quite a lot of travelling, indeed across to France for a holiday in Calais and getting somewhat smashed up and broken steering cable etc. in an unforecast force 7 gale off Margate. Ended up being towed in the dark from Sheerness up to Rochester and going through 6 foot high waves at Chatham. The trip back from Rochester to Teddington is another story but we made it. The boat was repaired and dried out and then we bought a Broom 30 with the kids around which had more space and cabins, then financial disaster and had to downsize and did a swap for a Seamaster 8 metre and then after a long period replaced by a Dutch 32 foot Linssen, built to our specification in Holland, then a Broads built boat 34 feet and then the last and current boat, Aquanaut 11.5 metres, built very much to our specification with 125 extras including a second engine which we've still got at the moment 17 years on and still looking pretty good. We're currently moored at the Upper Thames Club in Sonning where we had moored some 25 years previously then deserted to Phyllis Court Club in Henley but finding the cost of two moorings rather costly in recent years, returned back to Sonning. As I've said, pretty active in the club, having been the youngest Commodore ever and probably for a long time yet, in 1977, having been a club member and indeed involved since before the clubhouse was built and having used my surveying expertise on a number of occasions in saving the club fees and carrying out major repair and restoration works to the original clubhouse. This was in fact a second hand Blacknell timber school building dismantled and brought over from Camberley and about all that is left is the original floor of the original 30ft x 30ft building and part of one wall and the roof.

Just to give you the full picture, I have also been involved in shooting, mostly clays but for quite a while game as well, although currently two of my guns are up for sale to do a swap for a smaller and lighter 20 bore but my shooting days are very limited and it's expensive.

At Hillier Parker I formed a shooting club which at one time had about 100 members and with crack shots like Greg Nicholson in the team, we often did quite well in the Annual Property Gun and Punt Club competition, if I recall on one occasion getting 100 out of 100 on the flurry.

Well that's about the end. Still trying to work, in my 79th year but unfortunately major contracts don't come to one man bands!

Not much of a legacy to leave I'm afraid, still enjoying life at the moment but unfortunately finances won't stretch much beyond 10 years.